FORGOTTEN YOUTH

Child Soldiers

John Allen

ReferencePoint
Press®

San Diego, CA

LIBRARY OF CONGRESS CATALOGING-IN-PUBLICATION DATA

Name: Allen, John, 1957– author.
Title: Child soldiers by John Allen.
Description: San Diego, CA: ReferencePoint Press, Inc., [2017] | Series:
    Forgotten youth | Includes bibliographical references and index.
Identifiers: LCCN 2015044998 (print) | LCCN 2015045692 (ebook) | ISBN
    9781601529749 (hardback) | ISBN 9781601529756 (epub)
Subjects: LCSH: Child soldiers--History--21st century.
Classification: LCC UB416 .A86 2017 (print) | LCC UB416 (ebook) | DDC
    355.0083--dc23
LC record available at http://lccn.loc.gov/2015044998

Contents

Introduction

Sold into Service

Tun Tun Win was kicking a soccer ball with friends on a dusty lot in Myanmar (formerly Burma) when he was approached by a smiling stranger. The man praised the fourteen-year-old for his stamina and agility. Those qualities are valued in the military, he told the boy. He proceeded to describe the exciting life of a soldier in the Myanmar army: the weapons training and target practice, the camaraderie with other recruits, the chance to show a patriotic spirit. In short order Tun Tun was lured into the military and sold into service for the Tatmadaw, one of the largest armies in Southeast Asia. The stranger doubtless claimed his broker's fee for obtaining a new recruit. For the next several years, Tun Tun moved from base to base, helping repair tanks or taking security detail, all for about $4.50 a month. "I learned how to drive, shoot, do security, not much else,"[1] he says. Today at age thirty, Tun Tun has returned to his childhood village with little to show for his years in the army. Making use of one hundred dollars from an international relief group, he has started a makeshift library in front of his house, lending books and magazines for ten cents a day. His forced service robbed him of education and a possible career, but he displays no bitterness. "I want to be my own boss now," Tun Tun says. "I don't have any ill feelings toward army recruiters. Karma will be their judgment. I have freedom now. In the army I was renting out my body."[2]

A Worldwide Problem

Stories like Tun Tun's are not uncommon. Today an estimated three hundred thousand child soldiers are serving in armies around the world. Statistics on child soldiers and details about their daily routines remain elusive since few reporters or aid workers are able to gain entry into rebel camps. Child soldiers are mostly found in developing countries, particularly in sub-Saharan Africa, where almost two-thirds of contemporary conflicts rage. Underage soldiers exist in Somalia, Sudan, South Sudan, and the Democratic Republic of Congo in Africa. They also are found in Syria, Iraq, and Yemen in the Middle East, and in Colombia in South America. Wherever armed conflicts break out, whether due to failed states, civil wars, terrorist uprisings, or drug-crime cartels, children become vulnerable to recruitment and exploitation as fighters. Despite the development in the past thirty years of international legal standards to protect children, the chaos of war makes them very difficult to enforce.

> "I want to be my own boss now. . . . In the army I was renting out my body."[2]
>
> —Former Myanmar child soldier Tun Tun Win.

Like Tun Tun, many young people under age eighteen—the minimum allowed age for soldiers, according to international human rights law—are lured or abducted into service. Many more volunteer out of desperate circumstances of poverty or violence. Youths are pressed into service as fighters, guards, messengers, spies, cooks, porters, and servants. Some are forced to go on suicide missions or to act as sexual slaves. Child soldiers are associated in the public mind with rebel armies, but the governments of more than forty nations, including Myanmar, regularly recruit fighters under age eighteen. And not all child soldiers are male; some experts estimate that 30 to 40 percent of child soldiers are female.

Children in the Shadows

Child soldiers are not a new phenomenon. Yet tactics of modern warfare tend to make the problem worse. Increasingly, armed conflicts take place not on a battlefield but in and around crowded urban centers. In such circumstances children can easily be swept up into the fighting. Paramilitary or rebel groups use various methods for recruitment. Children whose families have been attacked or killed may join rebel forces from a desire for revenge, whereas others may be kidnapped or coerced into joining through threats of violence to family members. Some children are promised money, merchandise, or drugs if they join. Once in the fold, child soldiers often are brutalized into becoming ruthless fighters, willing to follow orders without question. They are valued as messengers and spies, able to slip unnoticed past enemy troops. Their nondescript innocence can make them prime candidates for sabotage or suicide bombings. Their slender fingers may prove useful in cleaning weapons or manipulating small parts. Yet when not fighting or working, these underage soldiers may long for a parent's embrace or simply to play games with other children.

Experts differ about the best ways to address the problem of child soldiers. Several international aid groups are devoted to helping child soldiers reintegrate into their villages or communities. However, studies show that former child soldiers face severe challenges in adjustment. Many suffer from post-traumatic stress disorder and other mental and emotional ailments. Recent reports from Iraq and Syria indicate that the insurgent group ISIS (Islamic State in Syria) is brainwashing children as young as age nine to become fanatical fighters against its supposed religious foes. This type of indoctrination is one more psychological hurdle to be overcome, should these children manage to escape their captors and return to normal society.

Like children around the world caught in webs of poverty or abuse, child soldiers often seem to fade into the shadows, unloved, misunderstood, and nearly forgotten. In recent years some former child soldiers, such as Ishmael Beah, have told their stories. Beah's book *A Long Way Gone: Memoirs of a Boy Solder* describes how he fell in with government troops in Sierra Leone at age thirteen. Beah's sometimes harrowing tale is typical of the plight of a child soldier—a homeless youth suddenly thrust into a life of violence. As childhood abuse expert Dave Pelzer says, "Childhood should be carefree, playing in the sun; not living a nightmare in the darkness of the soul."[3]

> "Childhood should be carefree, playing in the sun; not living a nightmare in the darkness of the soul."[3]
>
> —Childhood abuse expert Dave Pelzer.

Chapter 1

The Problem of Child Soldiers Today

The conflict in Syria, which began in late 2011, is a chaotic situation, with several different armed groups fighting to topple the regime of Syrian president Bashar al-Assad. The rebel armies and government forces do have one thing in common: They all use child soldiers. Human Rights Watch, an international monitoring group, found that opposition armies fighting government troops in Syria commonly use fighters as young as fifteen, and children even younger take support roles. Boys described to interviewers how they fought on the front lines, served as snipers, spied on government forces, treated the wounded in combat, and carried ammunition and supplies to support the battle effort. Extremist Islamist groups such as ISIS and Nusra Front were particularly aggressive in recruiting children. One doctor with Human Rights Watch reported treating a boy of about ten whose task was to whip prisoners held in an ISIS facility. Although overall numbers of child soldiers in Syria are hard to determine, a Syrian group has documented more than two hundred deaths of what it calls noncivilian male children—a vague reference to boy soldiers and support personnel. The group suspects the actual total is much higher.

An Urgent Problem in Several Countries

Human Rights Watch discovered that Syrian youth joined armed groups for various reasons. Some lived in battle zones where schools had closed, and were drawn into the fighting from lack of anything better to do. Some had suffered violence from government troops and joined the opposition seeking revenge. Others simply followed the lead of friends or relatives. Constant warfare had left many of the children numb to violence and blasé about the future—providing the warring parties with an underage army of nonchalant killers. "Maybe we'll live, and maybe we'll die,"[4] said Omar, who joined Nusra Front at age fourteen. Confronted about the recruitment of child soldiers like Omar, commanders among the armed groups insisted they are taking steps to end the practice. Yet youths continue to be drawn into the conflict.

The plight of child soldiers in Syria is not unique. A July 27, 2015, report by the US Department of State reveals that although recruitment of child soldiers is declining in some countries, it remains an urgent problem in many others. The report lists eight governments—Myanmar, the Democratic Republic of Congo, Nigeria, Somalia, South Sudan, Sudan, Syria, and Yemen—that recruit or use child soldiers in their own armed forces or back militias or other armed crews that include child soldiers. In 2014 only a single new child soldier was reportedly recruited in Congo—a vast improvement from past years—but military commanders there are said to provide money and equipment to freelance groups that continue to use children as fighters. Nigeria made the State Department's list for the first time, due to a government-backed militia called the Civilian Joint Task Force that recruits children to fight the Islamist militant group Boko Haram. South Sudan, which in recent years had made some progress in this area, saw widespread recruiting of child soldiers occur as fighting broke out anew at the end of 2013. In Yemen the Houthi rebel group that toppled the government in September 2014 uses child soldiers as a matter of course. In fact, the United Nations Children's Fund (UNICEF) estimates that up to one-third of the combatants in Yemen are children.

In an effort to halt the practice, the United States and other Western nations have sanctioned governments that recruit child soldiers, but as a practical matter these sanctions rarely last. In late September 2015, after much deliberation, President Barack

> ## "Maybe we'll live, and maybe we'll die."[4]
>
> —A child soldier named Omar who joined Nusra Front at age fourteen.

Obama announced that the United States will continue to provide military assistance to four countries (including Nigeria and South Sudan) that use child soldiers. "The decision is disappointing," says Jo Becker, director of the Children's Rights Division of Human Rights Watch, "particularly since Obama has a powerful tool at his disposal—the Child Soldiers Prevention Act—that allows him to withhold US military aid until governments end their exploitation of children in war."[5]

No Means of Escape

Despite the efforts of international organizations like Human Rights Watch and UNICEF, child soldiers remain a key component of warfare in the twenty-first century. UNICEF defines a child soldier as "any child—boy or girl—under 18 years of age, who is part of any kind of regular or irregular armed force or armed group in any capacity."[6] This definition shows that child soldiers are not only those who wield weapons or carry ammunition. Often they are forced to perform services for the group, including as cooks, porters (carriers of supplies and equipment), messengers, spies, smugglers, and even sexual slaves. Some child soldiers are recruited as young as age eight to fight in wars whose causes they barely understand. Once snared in the day-to-day operations of a rebel army, youths may find themselves with no means of escape.

The UN Convention on the Rights of the Child prohibits recruiting soldiers under age fifteen. Nevertheless, such recruiting continues in many battle-torn areas. Children are recruited to become soldiers for many reasons. They can more easily be conditioned to follow orders without question, and they can be brainwashed to express fanatical loyalty. They require less food and water than adults and may have little interest in payment. With their underdeveloped sense

"Due to their size and 'expendability,' children are often sent into battle as scouts or decoys, or sent in the first wave to draw the enemy's fire."[7]

—The international aid group War Child.

10

Reported Use of Child Soldiers, 2010–2015

The recruitment and use of child soldiers takes place in many countries. These child soldiers may serve in government armies, rebel militias, terrorist groups, and resistance forces. The map highlights countries in which child soldiers were reported between 2010 and 2015. The numbers in individual countries are hard to determine with accuracy, but experts estimate that more than 300,000 children are actively fighting in conflicts worldwide.

Source: CNN, "Child Soldier Use Around the World," April 29, 2015. www.cnn.com.

of danger, they more readily accept errands in the line of fire. And in many third world locations where conflicts arise, there is no shortage of children available to be exploited. According to the aid group War Child, "As children make the majority demographic in many conflict-affected countries, there's a constant supply of potential recruits. Due to their size and 'expendability,' children are often sent into battle as scouts or decoys, or sent in the first wave to draw the enemy's fire."[7] Living day to day, with no thought of the future, child soldiers may only seek the approval of their comrades and take great satisfaction in the feeling that they have done their part for the group. They tend to grow desensitized to violence and may become almost incapable of making moral judgments. Commanders value these hardened young fighters as versatile weapons of war.

Recruitment of child soldiers takes many forms. Some rebel groups, such as Joseph Kony's Lord's Resistance Army in Uganda, abduct children from their homes and force them into service. Rebel commanders may coerce villages to provide them with a quota of children in exchange for protection. Destitute parents may offer their children for food or money. Orphans may join out of an urge for revenge against the enemy soldiers who murdered their parents or family members—even though the actual murderers are sometimes their supposed rescuers. Older children may offer their services from patriotic feelings or ideological concerns. Some youths may want to escape abuse at home or simply seek thrills amid the surrounding chaos of civil war. Regardless of how they end up in armed groups, child soldiers usually find themselves trapped in a cycle of exploitation and abuse.

Child Soldiers in Africa

Although the recruitment and exploitation of child soldiers remains widespread, the problem is most severe across the African continent. There economic doldrums and political unrest repeatedly lead to armed revolts that draw children into the fighting. As elsewhere, most African nations have officially agreed to ban the use of child soldiers, ratifying the African Charter on the Rights and Welfare of the Child, for example. But although some progress has been made, the charters and agreements have failed to stop the practice. Andrew Friedman, a journalist and human rights attorney based in Africa, knows the problem has no simple solution. He says:

> The use of child soldiers is a scourge on society. In addition to the simple horror of forcing children, who should be playing and learning, to experience hell on earth, it prevents a generation from learning and working to end conflicts,

Displaced Sudanese families seek refuge from fighting taking place in Darfur. Refugee camps like this one, south of Darfur, have become fertile recruiting grounds for child soldiers.

perpetuating violence and discord. For this reason the use of child soldiers is illegal under international law. . . . However, it is an extremely difficult problem to deal with. Even as governments acknowledge its horror and work to end the practice, non-governmental entities, that often have no problem violating human rights norms, continue to kidnap, recruit and enlist children.[8]

Children with Kalashnikovs

In the city of Sanaa in northern Yemen, seven-year-old Hassan stands guard at a Houthi rebel-controlled checkpoint. His large dark eyes scrutinize each vehicle that passes through. Now and then he shifts the weight of his Kalashnikov rifle, a weapon that seems almost as tall as he is. Just three weeks ago Hassan was with classmates at school or laughing and playing table football with friends. That was before fighting between Houthi rebels and Saudi-backed government troops forced Hassan's school to close. Within days Hassan had abandoned his books for a rifle and a new job manning checkpoints and keeping watch for infiltrating enemy soldiers. He is eager to do his part for the rebels. "We are fighting to protect our country from the enemies," he declares.

Jamal al-Shami, head of the Democracy School, a local aid organization, blames both sides for the recruitment of child soldiers like Hassan. He notes that children are lured by the promise of money or told it is their duty to defend their tribal groups from outside aggression. As the fighting escalates, more young people find themselves drawn into the conflict. "Schools are closed and children have easy access to weaponry," says al-Shami. "All parties to the conflict have welcomed them with open arms. It's a mess." Millions of Yemeni children find themselves facing the same choices as Hassan. Eleven-year-old Asif carries a rifle and supports the Houthi cause without question. Asif says, "My parents are proud of me and encourage me to fight."

Quoted in Charlene Rodrigues and Mohammed Al-Qalisis, "Yemen Crisis: Meet the Child Soldiers Who Have Forsaken Books for Kalashnikovs," *Independent,* April 18, 2015. www.independent.co.uk.

A perfect example of the African dilemma regarding child soldiers is the nation of Chad in north central Africa, bounded to the east by Sudan and South Sudan. The region of Chad that borders Sudan is poor and politically unstable—a tinderbox for rebel violence. Since 2003 this region has been roiled by the conflict in neighboring Darfur, where rebels took up arms against the Sudanese government, claiming years of neglect. The violence sent hundreds of thousands of Darfuri refugees pouring across the border into eastern Chad. The Darfuris are held in refugee camps, while more than 170,000 Chadians have fled their homes to live in special sites for displaced persons.

In this chaotic situation, with almost a half million people marooned in temporary camps, armed opposition groups roam freely. The camps are viewed as fertile recruiting grounds for child soldiers. With almost no access to schools or jobs, the residents are desperate for a way out. Rebel groups send children dressed in new clothes into the camps to lure recruits with money—between $20 and $500—cigarettes, and promises of more bounty from looting. Those between the ages of thirteen and seventeen take up arms, while children as young as ten serve as messengers and porters. One former child soldier who fought with the Sudanese rebel group Justice and Equality Movement (JEM) and later returned to a camp in Chad explained to Amnesty International the allure of the rebel armies. "There is nothing to do here [in the camps]," he said. "There is no work, no school, no money and I am poor. . . . In the JEM I am not paid but, when we are in combat, we take stuff from the enemy."[9]

In 2011 Amnesty International issued a scathing report about the situation in Chad. More than forty former and current child soldiers from Chad and Darfur described how they were forced to join rebel groups. The Chadian government was criticized for giving amnesty to opposition groups accused of war crimes, including the recruitment of child soldiers. "It is tragic that thousands of children are denied their childhood and are manipulated by adults into fighting their wars," said Erwin van der Borght, Amnesty International's program director for Africa. "This scandalous child abuse must not be allowed to continue."[10] Perhaps in response to Amnesty International's exposé, Chad's government has made some progress in addressing the problem. In 2014 the UN removed Chad from its list of violators that engage in or enable the recruitment of child soldiers.

The Plight of Girl Soldiers
Armed groups also do not hesitate to recruit or abduct girls as soldiers and support personnel. Experts estimate that 30 to 40

percent of child soldiers are female. With the advent of lightweight weapons such as the AK-47 rifle, young females are fully capable of taking part in combat. Like male child soldiers, females who are abducted by rebels often are beaten, rapidly trained to fire a weapon, and forced to serve in the front lines on deadly missions. They may be used as human shields or decoys in an ambush. Many combine their fighting role with duties such as cooking, cleaning, and laundering in the rebel camps. Girls may become trusted fighters in the close-knit rebel bands, where group safety depends on each soldier's prowess. Ironically, some girl soldiers may experience something that was rare in their home life: equality with males. According to a Care International report on child soldiers in Colombia, "For some girls, belonging to an illegal armed group gives them a sense of power and control that they may not otherwise experience living in a relatively conservative, 'machista' [chauvinist] society."[11] Such hints of equality pale before the hardships suffered by a girl soldier forced into service, robbed of her childhood, and indoctrinated to violence.

> "Many of these girls had to give birth while in captivity, some of them had to go fighting with children on their backs, and some gave birth on the battlefield."[12]
>
> —Grace Akallo, who was abducted by Ugandan rebels as a young girl.

Faced with imminent death on the battlefield, females are also vulnerable to another aspect of the child soldier's life: sexual abuse. Girls are frequently taken as sexual slaves to serve the whims of a commander. Some are assigned as camp wives to other soldiers. Few female child soldiers escape sexual abuse of some kind. Thus, they run the risk of getting pregnant at an early age—and possibly having to undergo a brutal abortion—as well as contracting AIDS or some other disease. Grace Akallo, who was abducted by Ugandan rebels as a young girl, has testified to the sexual abuse she and other young girls suffered. "Most girls were sexually abused, including me," says Akallo. "I was lucky I did not return home with a child, or get infected with HIV or any other disease. . . . Many of these girls had to give birth while in captivity, some of them had to go fighting with children on their backs, and some gave birth on the battlefield."[12]

Many experts believe girl child soldiers have been overlooked in efforts to police the problem and return child soldiers to society. Those who serve in roles other than fighting may be ignored by disarmament programs focused on soldiers who turn in weapons. Armed rebel groups and militias are rarely prosecuted for rape and sexual abuse of female child soldiers, even when these crimes are obvious and rampant. Returning a former

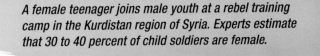

A female teenager joins male youth at a rebel training camp in the Kurdistan region of Syria. Experts estimate that 30 to 40 percent of child soldiers are female.

Girl Soldiers in Sierra Leone

In 1991 the African nation of Sierra Leone exploded into a bloody civil war. The war continued for eleven years and left fifty thousand dead. During the conflict, thousands of children were abducted by rebel armies and forced to fight. More than a third were females. In 2014 South African filmmaker Jonathan Torgovnik spent a week with some of these females in their home village.

Their stories demonstrate how girls, no less than boys, suffer from the experience of being child soldiers. One young woman named Mabinti was abducted by rebels at age twelve and constantly drugged. She described how she would cut off the hands and ears of dead victims. Under duress, Mabinti would also use powerful glue to clamp prisoners' eyelids shut or seal their lips so that they could not speak. Sally, who was abducted at age eleven, was handed a gun she could scarcely drag along the ground. After repeated beatings, she began to follow orders to kill. At age twelve, Laura watched rebels burn her home to the ground on Christmas morning. She and her sisters were then raped and taken to a rebel camp in the forest. Janet was forced to serve as the sex slave of a rebel leader. "And when the war ended," she recalls, "we came out to the town, he left me here. He never came again." Villagers shunned Janet, now with a child, as a rebel's concubine. Like the other girls, Janet faced a difficult recovery from her trauma.

Quoted in Jonathan Torgovnik, "Girl Soldier: Stories from a Civil War," MSNBC, March 4, 2014. www.msnbc.com.

female child soldier to her home village may be complicated by many factors—for example, the girl may have an unwanted baby whom neighbors view sourly as a sign of collaboration with the enemy. The stigma may force a young woman, already shell-shocked from years of violence and abuse, to abandon her childhood home. Such females desperately need counseling, education, and job training in order to change their lives. An unfortunate number, however, turn to prostitution to support themselves and their children.

Reintegrating Child Soldiers into Society

Both male and female child soldiers face steep challenges in trying to reintegrate back into society. Since 1998 UNICEF and other international relief groups have had some success helping child soldiers return home and start down the path to recovery. Whereas the reintegration process used to focus on the child's physical needs, such as food, water, shelter, security, and family reunification, now more emphasis is placed on mental and emotional adjustment. Experts realize that former child soldiers must often deal with symptoms of post-traumatic stress disorder, which may include nightmares, flashbacks, and feelings of hopelessness, guilt, fear, and anxiety. They must overcome the stigma attached to their former life and reestablish bonds of trust and respect with family members, friends, and neighbors. Today peace accords in regional conflicts often include provisions for psychiatric examination and care to aid child soldiers in the transition back to a normal life.

Above all, the problem of child soldiers must be dragged into the light and given the attention it deserves. Too many people in war-torn regions accept the recruitment and use of child soldiers with a shrug, pleading that the unending chaos and violence make it impossible to stop the practice. Too many children who should be in school or on a playground instead are wearing oversize camouflage fatigues and brandishing high-powered weapons with a cold look in their eyes. "What has humanity created?" asks Roméo Dallaire, a former leader of the UN peacekeeping force in the 1994 Rwandan genocide. "What have we permitted to be created? Alive and breathing in the hundreds of thousands in not-so-far-off lands are beings who have the physical form of children, yet who have been robbed of the spirit, the innocence, the essence of childhood. . . . Where do we go from here?"[13]

Chapter 2

Recruiting Children to Fight

In January 2015 the Nigerian Islamist terror group Boko Haram tweeted out photographs of a training camp for recent recruits. The photos showed ranks of children, some obviously younger than ten years old. They were expressionless, wearing keffiyehs (loose head scarves) and dark tunics and wielding semiautomatic rifles. The images confirmed what Human Rights Watch spokespeople had been warning for some time: that Boko Haram was kidnapping boys and girls and using them in attacks against the Nigerian government. These so-called Cubs of the Caliphate—youths exploited in the attempt to establish by force a new kingdom of Islam—would soon be thrown in the line of fire by rebel commanders. The tweeted photos offered further proof of Boko Haram's ruthless tactics toward children.

Exploitation on Both Sides

Boko Haram, like rebel armies and terrorist bands elsewhere in Africa and in other parts of the world, insists on recruiting children and forcing them to serve as soldiers. Watchlist on Children and Armed Conflict, an international research group, estimates that 40 percent of Boko Haram's sixty thousand troops are children. Boko Haram's insurgency began in 2009, but the group first drew international attention in April 2014 after it seized two hundred schoolgirls in the northern village of Chibok. The kidnapping led to a high-profile worldwide campaign—dubbed #BringBackOurGirls—seeking the girls' release. In the meantime, Boko Haram's leader, Abubakar Shekau, declared that the abducted girls had immediately converted to Islam—doubtless without a choice. Shortly before the training camp photos appeared, Boko Haram soldiers reportedly kidnapped at least thirty more children in another northern village, including girls as young as eleven. The children were forced either to take up arms or suffer the consequences—beatings or even death. Pastor Laolu Akande, executive director of a large Nigerian church organization, has called on the world community to help stop the kidnappings and stem the tide of violence. "Boko Haram members are very despicable and brutal," Akande says, "and every person in the world has to rise and say no to this violence."[14]

Villages in northern Nigeria have organized armed militias to fight Boko Haram. A teenage boy named Aliko was recruited by one of these pro-government militias, called the Civilian Joint Task Force, in the northeast city of Maidiguri. Aliko faced a simple choice: Either join the fight against Boko Haram or become one of their victims. Aliko is only fourteen years old, and he should be attending school and playing games with classmates. Instead, he is a soldier—alert, efficient, deadly serious, with the arrest of dozens of Boko Haram insurgents to his credit. One night he tied two captured terrorists together and guarded them for hours before turning them over to military authorities at dawn. Aliko and other child soldiers make up nearly a quarter of the ten thousand strong self-defense brigades fighting Boko Haram. Militia leaders insist that using child soldiers is necessary to counter the terrorists' increasingly frequent attacks. "The insurgents are many in number, and we need as many people as we can get to fight them," says Bukkar, one of the older militia members. "These kids have lots of energy and are very important in this fight."[15] Others, however, lament the war's effect on the lives of their children. "We've lost our kids to the war," says Shettima Kunduli, a local leader in Maidiguri. "Our young ones are no longer children, they are commanders

> "We've lost our kids to the war. Our young ones are no longer children, they are commanders who despite their brave efforts have lost their childhood, their education, and maybe their future."[16]
>
> —Shettima Kunduli, a local leader in the northern Nigerian city of Maidiguri.

21

who despite their brave efforts have lost their childhood, their education, and maybe their future."[16]

Young people in northern Nigeria suffer exploitation from both sides of the conflict. Whether abducted by Boko Haram or forcibly recruited by pro-government militias, they are in danger of having their childhood years snatched away. Should they survive the war, they will face at best a future filled with hardship and uncertainty. Hardened by constant fighting, lacking education and culture, sometimes lacking even the basic skills of reading and arithmetic, these child soldiers seem destined to become a lost generation.

Recruitment and Kidnapping

Children become soldiers mostly in so-called failed states—countries or regions where the government has broken down and can no longer maintain order. Often these are developing coun-

At a 2015 rally, activists call on the Nigerian government to do more to rescue more than two hundred girls kidnapped by the violent Boko Haram group. Both Boko Haram and armed militias fighting the group are recruiting child soldiers.

tries where families are large and many children grow up impoverished, undernourished, and with limited access to schools. A harried government struggles to keep track of voting-age citizens, let alone their offspring, and orphans are often unaccounted for.

Armed rebellion against the government may be based on economic grievances, racial hatred, or religious strife. When states break apart into armed factions or erupt into civil war, the resulting violence tends to be especially brutal and intense. Norms that are taken for granted in peaceable times—such as the responsibility of adults to protect children at all costs—can vanish entirely when war breaks out. Poverty and violence create desperation, leading people to act against their own best interests and those of their society. In such chaotic circumstances, militia leaders and warlords come to view children as easily available and useful weapons of war. Should they be wounded or killed, there are always plenty more to be exploited. As war correspondent Jeffrey Gettleman notes, "Today's rebels seem especially uninterested in winning converts, content instead to steal other people's children, stick Kalashnikovs or axes in their hands, and make them do the killing."[17]

The methods of recruiting child soldiers are as various as the conflicts into which they are thrown. Some children are lured into fighting with promises of food, money, drugs, or shares in looting. Youths living in grinding poverty may be easily swayed by the prospect of pocket money and regular meals. Some are indoctrinated to the rebels' cause through their schools. This method of recruitment has been used effectively by the Tamil Tigers, a rebel movement in Sri Lanka, which has also seized thousands of young people by force. Some children are blackmailed into joining a militia with threats to

> "Today's rebels seem especially uninterested in winning converts, content instead to steal other people's children, stick Kalashnikovs or axes in their hands, and make them do the killing."[17]
>
> —War correspondent Jeffrey Gettleman.

their parents or siblings. Some are forced to murder a parent or relative to ensure that they can never return to their families. Many children are abducted at gunpoint and hauled away to be trained in the use of rifles, grenades, and bayonets. In the early 2000s, Revolutionary United Front (RUF) rebels in Sierra Leone commonly kidnapped children for use as soldiers or to carry equipment and looted goods. RUF soldiers also abducted and raped young girls, forcing them later to serve as cooks or servants.

When the government in Sierra Leone created demobilization camps for child soldiers who had managed to escape, RUF troops would infiltrate and try to rerecruit the youths back to the insurgency. The surrounding disorder and lack of security enabled the rebels to prey upon young camp residents. They would threaten to kill everyone in the camp if a child refused to go with them, or they would make false promises to reunite a child with his or her parents. Some RUF soldiers spread rumors in the camps that the government planned to sell them into slavery. Time and again camps set up in war-torn lands for refugees or former soldiers end up being fertile grounds for recruiting or rerecruiting child soldiers.

Abduction in Uganda

In northern Uganda, the warlord Joseph Kony and his Lord's Resistance Army (LRA) have relied chiefly on force to add children to their ranks. LRA soldiers often forced young recruits to murder their parents, leaving the children with no family to return to. Kony's men also employed brainwashing techniques. Norman, a boy of twelve, was accompanying his father back to their village when they were suddenly surrounded by five LRA soldiers. The soldiers, sporting ragged dreadlocks and uniforms stolen from the Ugandan army, repeatedly asked Norman if the man was his father. Repeatedly, he denied it. He knew that if he acknowledged his father, the soldiers would demand that he kill him. The soldiers finally took father and son to their commander. As his father was forced to watch, Norman was brutally beaten by teenagers wielding heavy sticks. Bloodied, racked with pain, and dressed only in his school shorts, Norman was led away into confinement.

Girls Recruited as Guerrilla Fighters

Many young girls are abducted by armed groups or lured into joining militias. Whether these girls take up arms in combat depends on the nature of their captors and the area where the conflict takes place. Many African and Middle Eastern groups enslave young females for domestic work or sexual exploitation. A group of Marxist guerrillas in Colombia, however, often trains abducted girls to be fighters no different from their male counterparts. The Revolutionary Armed Forces of Colombia (FARC), a notoriously ruthless rebel army, forces girls to undergo grueling military training and to fight on the front lines in their longtime insurgency against the Colombian government. Girls are taught to fire pistols and AK-47 assault rifles and learn to assemble and lay homemade land mines. They also must prove themselves capable of enduring weeks-long marches through the mountains while carrying packs of heavy equipment. Some operate radio communications for guerrilla commanders hidden in the jungle and help recruit other child soldiers from neighboring villages.

For years the FARC has financed its rebellion with criminal operations such as cocaine trafficking, kidnapping, and extortion. Here young girls have proved themselves especially useful to the group. One former girl soldier told the BBC, "The FARC really wanted to recruit [girls] for this reason, because no one suspects a little girl. A little girl can transport money, weapons, drugs much more easily." Once implicated in the group's crimes, young female recruits find it even more difficult to escape.

Quoted in Brigit Katz, "Female Child Soldiers Can Be Victims of Abuse, Perpetrators of Violence," Women in the World and *New York Times*, August 4, 2015. http://nytlive.nytimes.com.

Certain that his father was dead (although, in fact, his father had survived), Norman saw his situation as hopeless.

Three days later the soldiers forced Norman to march for hours with other new recruits. The LRA men told the boys they were unclean and did not deserve to take meals with the regular soldiers. When finally allowed to eat with the LRA troops, Norman felt relieved and elated. He continued to receive harsh treatment interspersed with occasional tokens of favor. Two months later an LRA commander forced Norman and some other newcomers to murder an eighteen-year-old escaped prisoner with clubs, machetes, and bayonets. "When you kill for the first time, automatically, you change," Norman says. "Out of being innocent, you've now become guilty. You feel like you're becoming part of them, part of the rebels."[18] Over weeks filled with bullying, beatings, and murderous raids on villages, Norman transferred his loyalty to the LRA. He came to believe in the supremacy of Kony, the rebels' messianic leader, who claimed to be possessed by powerful ghosts. Soon Norman was taking part in abductions and assaults on new recruits. His days were filled with rage and despair.

Years later he finally escaped and turned himself in to the Ugandan military, which transferred him to a psychiatric treatment center near his home village. When his mother got word of his return, she rushed to see him. However, with his swollen shaved head, bloodshot eyes crusty with conjunctivitis, and stomach bloated from hunger, she did not recognize him. When he was able to return home, his angry outbursts made it difficult for him to adapt to normal life. Only after years of therapy was Norman able to accept a simple message: It was not his fault. Today Norman is happily married with two children of his own. "I'm normal now," he says. "I'm just another member of the community. But the nightmare is there. I dream about someone coming to abduct me."[19]

Going from the Classroom to the Front Line

By 2015 Kony and his LRA forces, reduced to about two hundred combatants, had fled Uganda for the border region of Congo and South Sudan. While Kony's recruitment of child soldiers has declined, it has continued to increase among the warring militants across the border in South Sudan. There children and their families are caught up in the conflict between government forces loyal to President Salva Kiir and rebels ruled by former vice president Riek Machar. According to Human Rights Watch, both sides are guilty of recruiting and using child soldiers as young as twelve. In 2011, when the country claimed its independence from Sudan, its national army, the Sudan People's Liberation Army, swore to end its long-standing practice of using child soldiers. In August 2013, amid a period of relative calm, army commanders announced a general order forbidding the recruitment of children younger than eighteen for any operational use. In December 2013, however, civil war erupted in South Sudan, and child recruitment resumed at once. Since then, international monitoring groups have claimed that thousands of children are serving in various armed factions in South Sudan.

According to UNICEF, one of the chief culprits is Johnson Oloni, a militia leader from Upper Nile State whose forces are loyal to the government in South Sudan. In February 2015 Oloni's fighters seized more than one hundred students from a school complex in the community of Wau Shilluk in Upper Nile State. Militants apparently searched the school from building to building to take the young people by force. Witnesses soon afterward reported seeing the children carrying guns in a training camp not far from Wau Shilluk. Despite the difficulty of gathering information in the midst of armed militias, UNICEF investigators strive to monitor the children's plight. Apparently, the kidnapped children are not held in a single group. Some are even allowed back into their village to eat with their parents and in some cases permitted to go back to school for a short time. Then, at the whim of commanders, they are taken away again at night. Faced with the militants' threats, the children's parents and teachers are helpless to stop the abductions. Jonathan Veitch, UNICEF's representative in South Sudan, suspects the child soldiers are dispatched in boats to fight rebels at a town about forty-five minutes away. "We fear they are

"I'm normal now. I'm just another member of the community. But the nightmare is there. I dream about someone coming to abduct me."[19]

—Norman, a Ugandan boy who was abducted by LRA fighters at age twelve.

going from the classroom to the front line,"[20] says Veitch. When pressed about Oloni's use of child soldiers, Kiir insisted that the government has no control over the militia's actions.

South Sudan is another place where tumultuous civil war and overcrowded refugee camps combine to make the problem of child soldier recruitment much worse. Soon after the conflict began, it spread to the town of Malakal in Upper Nile State. Since then, the town has changed hands six times between government forces and the opposition. Near Malakal, the UN established a Protection of Civilians base, which has grown to house about twenty thousand refugees. Outside the gate of the camp is a busy market area that also serves as prime recruiting grounds for soldiers. Witnesses interviewed by Human Rights Watch report having seen militia soldiers, armed and unarmed, a few in uniforms, targeting men and boys for recruitment. Some recruits

Women and children wait in line for food at a refugee camp near war-torn Malakal in South Sudan in 2015. Just outside the camp young boys have been taken by force or voluntarily joined militias in hopes of getting paid work.

are taken by force or with threats of violence, while others join voluntarily in hopes of getting paid work. Typical of the abducted recruits is a young man who was picked up in Malakal and thrown into the back of a truck with six children, each apparently between the ages of thirteen and fifteen. He and the children were then driven to an area where fighting had broken out. "When we got to Koka [the battle area] we were told to go to fight, given weapons, and [ordered to] attack together with other soldiers," reported the young man after being freed. "We were given uniforms, almost immediately told to fight . . . all of us."[21]

Luring Recruits with Online Campaigns

Some groups have added more modern recruiting methods to tactics of brutal abduction or threats of violence. The terror group Islamic State, or ISIS, has launched an online campaign to lure young recruits with slickly produced propaganda videos. The videos and accompanying photos present the terrorists of ISIS as successful warriors armed with advanced weapons and bent on bringing fundamentalist Islam to the Middle East and the rest of the world. One video that appeared in the summer of 2015 was said to have been made in Mosul, Iraq, but was targeted at parents and children in Great Britain. With Hollywood-like production values, the seven-minute video depicts ISIS recruits as young as eleven dressed in combat gear and firing machine guns. One scene shows six child soldiers, their heads covered in black balaclavas (cloth headgear that exposes only part of the face), fighting each other inside a circular chainlink cage situated in a large warehouse. The youths square off in pairs and trade kicks and punches while a gun-wielding

"When we got to Koka [the battle area] we were told to go to fight, given weapons, and [ordered to] attack together with other soldiers. We were given uniforms, almost immediately told to fight . . . all of us."[21]

—A young man abducted by rebels in South Sudan.

instructor barks encouragement. Other soldiers in identical uniforms and masks ring the outside of the cage, their arms linked shoulder to shoulder in a show of solidarity. Flying above the cage are the black banners with Arabic inscriptions associated with ISIS. Other scenes show the instructor whacking and prodding the young recruits with a stick as they perform calisthenics or climb along the rungs of a gym apparatus. The instructor also has his charges smash stacks of clay tiles with their bare fists, as in a karate film. Throughout the video there is a keening sound track of hypnotic Arabic music and chanting.

Fighting for Money

Officials at UNICEF estimate that one-third of the fighters in the Middle Eastern nation of Yemen are children. An increasing number of these youths are lured to join warring militias with promises of cash payments and regular meals. Julien Harneis, the Yemen representative for UNICEF, sees armed groups in the nation's civil war targeting underage recruits in poverty-stricken areas. "Becoming a fighter is seen as a way to make money to survive for those children who come from vulnerable backgrounds," Harneis says. "And this is happening in all groups, from the north to south, in every corner of the country."

Battles between the rebel Houthi forces and government troops have plunged the country into turmoil. As more schools shut down due to the violence, the pool of potential child recruits continues to grow. With food and fuel increasingly scarce, many families are forced to rely on their children as breadwinners. Child soldiers can earn as much as one hundred dollars a month—a hefty sum in a country where half the population scraped by on two dollars a day even before the outbreak of civil war. Typical is Ayman, a scrawny seventeen-year-old who guards a Houthi-run military post for a salary of three dollars a day. His explanation for joining the rebels is quite simple: "There was nothing else for me to do."

Quoted in Ali al-Mujahed and Hugh Naylor, "In Yemen, Children—Possibly Thousands of Them—Join Fight," *Washington Post*, May 11, 2015. www.washingtonpost.com.

Islamic State (ISIS) fighters wave the group's flag during a military parade in Syria in 2014. The militant Islamist group has launched a slick online propaganda campaign to lure young recruits.

The message to parents is that ISIS will develop their children into effective soldiers for the jihad, or holy war, against the enemies of Islam. Professor Anthony Glees, director of Buckingham University's Centre for Security and Intelligence Studies, compares the video to Nazi leader Adolf Hitler's propaganda film *Triumph of the Will.* "This is sickening brutalization of kids for [Islamic State]," he says. "It is designed to appeal to mothers and fathers but children are also the target. The government must act."[22] Yet governments in the West have little recourse when recruiting videos appear online. Too many parents are persuaded to let their children take up arms in some supposed great cause. Whether snatched by kidnappers in a failed state or lured with elaborate videos promising military glory, young people continue to be vulnerable to recruitment as child soldiers.

Chapter 3

Life of a Child Soldier

Before the outbreak of war in Syria early in 2011, Majed, then thirteen, worked at farming tomatoes in fields outside his hometown of Inkhil in the southwestern part of the country. The boy's life changed when a militia group named the Nusra Front appeared in his town. Majed, along with other children the same age or younger, began spending time in a neighborhood mosque with soldiers from the group. "They would bring a car and go around to houses to pick up children," Majed recalls. "They taught children how to read the Quran, then taught us about weapon(s). They taught us how to take apart and put together a weapon, they put up a target for us to practice shooting outside the mosque. Anyone who hit the target got a reward."[23] Soon Majed had joined the Nusra Front and its battle against the government forces of Syrian president Bashar al-Assad. For months he led the life of a soldier in the field, despite the fact that he was still only a child. Amr, a fifteen-year-old living in northern Syria, followed a similar path. A radical Islamist group convinced the reluctant Amr to join their rebellion. When the commanders of his unit began lining up volunteers for suicide bombing attacks, Amr reconsidered. He was barely able to escape before it was his turn to strap on a vest filled with explosives.

Traumatic Changes to Daily Life

Suicide bomber is only one of the roles regularly assumed by underage combatants. In Syria, as in many other war-torn locales, young people are recruited to perform all the tasks of the regular frontline soldier. Minors—officially individuals under age eighteen—are found in both pro- and anti-government units—this despite the fact that international law forbids the recruitment and use of minors as soldiers. In many agrarian societies, the conception of childhood is different from that in Western countries. Developing nations often consider a person who is capable of doing adult work or has completed cultural rituals signifying adulthood to be no longer a child, regardless of age.

"At the end of the day, if they can carry a gun and are willing to fight, who are we to say they can't?"[24] said Ayman al-Hariri, a recruiter for Syrian opposition groups. Syrian children also fight alongside older relatives and neighbors in independent militias formed to defend home districts from marauding armed groups on both sides. Whatever their affiliation, children in Syria are employed as infantry or foot soldiers, snipers, suicide bombers, saboteurs, spies, guards, messengers, smugglers, carriers of equipment and supplies, medical assistants, and kitchen workers. Underage Syrian girls are often seized and forced to perform support roles behind the lines. Some are made to wed older soldiers or kept as sexual slaves.

"At the end of the day, if they can carry a gun and are willing to fight, who are we to say they can't?"[24]

—Ayman al-Hariri, a recruiter for Syrian opposition groups.

Syria today is a perfect example of how warfare can instantly change people's daily lives, especially those of young people. One day boys in a Syrian town such as Douma, 6 miles (10 km) northeast of Damascus, might be riding their bicycles or kicking a soccer ball for fun. Then soldiers from one of the armed rebel groups arrive in trucks and armored vehicles to seize control of the town. Within days or weeks the government responds with air attacks to drive out the opposition fighters. Shells and barrel bombs (containers packed with crude explosives and shrapnel) reduce buildings and homes to rubble, killing or wounding civilians, separating families, and sending desperate refugees in search of safer territory.

In the ensuing chaos, boys may latch onto a militia group to save themselves or to earn a bit of money. Soon they are

In 2015 two young members of the Nusra Front prepare to fire a mortar at forces loyal to Syria's president. Underage combatants in Syria and elsewhere fight on the front lines, function as suicide bombers, and more.

undergoing rudimentary training as soldiers or support personnel. They must quickly adapt to harsh military discipline. Forced to learn how to load and shoot a rifle, they nervously await their first trial by fire. Brandishing a weapon and following their commander's orders becomes second nature to boys who only a short time before were content to ride bikes and trade jokes with their friends. Their lives for the foreseeable future will be filled with the boredom of hiding out and performing menial chores and the anxiety of preparing for combat, punctuated by sudden spasms of violence and bloodshed. Experience in the field and daily contact with adult fighters hardens these youths, encourages them to be cynical about the world, and robs them of innocence. School is long forgotten. Teachers who once might have civilized the boys' outlook are nowhere to be found, replaced by militia leaders who brutally insist on obedience and sacrifice. Should these children somehow survive the ordeal, they will face the challenge of returning to ordinary life with traumatic memories and few prospects for the future.

Young People as Fighting Tools

Rebel militias in Syria and elsewhere value child soldiers for many reasons. Chief among these is the relative ease of programming children to become ruthless fighters. Commanders often take advantage of children's vulnerability and desire to belong, conditioning them to support the group without question. Some child soldiers are indoctrinated by force, suffering beatings or torture to instill the proper level of fear. Children may be given food, drugs, cash, or trinkets to secure their loyalty. Jo Becker, who has interviewed many former child soldiers for Human Rights Watch, points out that youths tend to be easy to manipulate. Their value systems and morals are not fully formed, leading them to perform even atrocious acts without protest. Armed warfare can seem like a game to some child soldiers. They delight in taking macho names like Colonel Rambo or Brigadier Chop-Them-Up. Children wielding guns almost taller than they are can be molded into alarmingly cold, effective fighters. Angela, a girl of twelve in Colombia, was ordered by FARC guerrillas to shoot a friend. "I closed my eyes and fired the gun, but I didn't hit her. So I shot again," she says. "I had to bury her and put dirt on top of her. The commander said, 'You'll have to do this many more times, and you'll have to learn not to cry.'"[25]

> "I had to bury her and put dirt on top of her. The commander said, 'You'll have to do this many more times, and you'll have to learn not to cry.'"[25]
>
> —Angela, a Colombian girl ordered by rebels to kill a friend.

Jeff Koinange, a CNN correspondent in Africa, knows the terror of facing child soldiers conditioned to be killers. While covering a rebel uprising in Freetown, Sierra Leone, a competitor's television crew was passing a checkpoint guarded by a group of very young soldiers. Suddenly, without warning, the boys opened fire on the crew, killing the crew chief and seriously wounding another man. Reflecting on the incident, Koinange says:

> That day taught each of us what a child soldier is capable of. . . . Each time I was around them I felt one step away from death. One wrong move and they can turn from innocent-looking children to killers. . . . At the end of the day, these children are victims of older soldiers, forced into war out of personal circumstances or peer pressure. . . . Once they're given an AK-47 and drugs, their innocence is lost, replaced by a killer instinct. . . . Killing becomes second nature and doesn't stop until the killer is stopped. And that's how many child soldiers end up—dead and mostly forgotten.[26]

Boys play soccer in the Syrian city of Aleppo, which has been the site of intense fighting. When family members are killed or separated from each other, children sometimes latch onto a militia group to save themselves or to earn money.

Child soldiers also are valued for taking orders without hesitation. Questions of strategy and psychology hold little interest for them, only the practical aspects of doing what they are told. Since they are less capable of evaluating the risks of combat, they often prove to be fearless fighters. Once indoctrinated, child soldiers tend to be intensely loyal to their commanders and units. And in regions such as Africa and the Middle East with high birth rates, children are found in almost endless supply, and thus are easily replaced when wounded or killed. They require less food and water than adults and are more susceptible to threats and punishment for discipline.

Dangerous Duty and Suicidal Risks

Commanders in rebel groups or government armies regularly employ child soldiers for the most dangerous duties. Their easy availability enables them to be exploited as so-called cannon fodder, forced to take suicidal risks as a matter of course. Militia leaders in many conflicts use children as decoys to draw enemy fire and discover their positions. Children posing as civilians act as messengers or spies, hoping to slip unnoticed through enemy territory, risking certain death if discovered. Child soldiers are often pushed to the front of an offensive operation and forced to endure the brunt of an enemy counterattack. In its war with Iraq in the 1980s, Iran sacrificed as many as one hundred thousand child soldiers by sending them to the front lines to attack in waves. Allegedly, each of these Iranian children wore a plastic key around his neck, a token issued by the Ayatollah signifying the key to paradise should the underage soldier meet his death on the battlefield. The wave attacks were largely futile. However, they did exact a psychological toll on the Iraqis, who were often hesitant to shoot

"Killing becomes second nature and doesn't stop until the killer is stopped. And that's how many child soldiers end up—dead and mostly forgotten."[26]

—Jeff Koinange, a CNN correspondent in Africa.

and took little satisfaction in mowing down children. As one Iraqi officer explained:

> [The child soldiers] chant "Allahu Akbar" [God is great] and they keep coming, and we keep shooting, sweeping our machine guns around like sickles. My men are eighteen, nineteen, just a few years older than these kids. I've seen them crying, and at times the officers have had to kick them [to make them shoot]. . . . Once we had Iranian kids on bikes cycling toward us, and my men started laughing, and then these kids started lobbing their hand grenades and we stopped laughing and started shooting.[27]

The Iranians also sent child soldiers marching into minefields to clear a safe path for their adult comrades. A sudden explosion would produce clouds of dust and leave only scraps of flesh and bone. Some child members of a volunteer militia began to wrap themselves in blankets before rolling onto a minefield, in hopes of keeping their body parts together for burial purposes in case of an explosion.

A Child Soldier's Experience in Sierra Leone

The danger and brutality of a child soldier's daily life are detailed in Ishmael Beah's *A Long Way Gone: Memoirs of a Boy Soldier*. When civil war broke out in 1991 in Sierra Leone, rebels overran Beah's hometown of Mogbwemo in the southern province. Amid the violence, Beah's parents and brother lost their lives, and he was forced to flee into the countryside. For months he wandered south, sometimes with a group of boys, his pockets filled with rap cassettes, his survival dependent on the charity of strangers along the way. At age thirteen he was captured and forced at gunpoint to join the Sierra Leone government army in its fight against rebel forces. At the village encampment, he was presented with an AK-47 and a new T-shirt and camouflage shorts. What he really prized, however, was his new Reebok sneakers. Soon he was

Coercion and Abuse

Army commanders or rebel leaders often employ physical abuse and intimidation with child soldiers. Because captured children are physically and psychologically vulnerable, abuse or the threat of force is an easy way to make them obey orders. New child recruits often are tested with grueling jobs, such as hauling supplies, which leave them exhausted. The slightest infraction can lead to beatings, whippings, caning, or being tied up or chained for several days. Commanders use threats of violence not only against the children but against their families or friends to coerce their obedience. Child soldiers are often ordered to assist in punishing or torturing other soldiers accused of mutiny or desertion. The idea is to keep child recruits steeped in fear and guilt and mindful of what could happen to them should they get out of line.

The national army of Myanmar punishes a child trainee by parading him through the ranks of fellow recruits, who take turns beating him with bamboo sticks while officers and other soldiers pin him down. Sai Seng was a seventeen-year-old trainee who was forced to participate in one of these sessions. "I felt pity on my friend so I hit him lightly," says Seng, "and the NCO came and said, 'Don't hit like that, hit like this' and hit me, and then made me hit my friend again." Beaten bloody until the sticks snapped from the force of the blows, Seng's friend died that same night.

Human Rights Watch, "Coercion and Intimidation of Child Soldiers to Participate in Violence," April 16, 2008. www.hrw.org.

deep in training with the other captive recruits, learning to crawl quickly and soundlessly through the trees and thick brush. After long hours of instruction on dismantling, oiling, reassembling, and firing his rifle, his trigger finger throbbed, his arms ached, and his ears still rang with the gun's loud reports.

A lieutenant stoked the recruits' hatred for the enemy rebels with a speech about their crimes, which included burning entire villages and their inhabitants, beheading people in front of their families, and hacking newborn babies in two. Beah and

A militia group made up of teen boys patrols the streets of their town in a northern province of Sierra Leone. Young recruits are easily influenced by adults who belittle, threaten, and manipulate them.

the others were told that the rebels did not deserve to live, that every one of them must be destroyed. Beah recalls:

> All of us hated the rebels, and we were more than determined to stop them from capturing the village. Everyone's face had begun to sadden and grow tense. The aura in the village rapidly changed after the speech. The morning sun had disappeared and the day became gloomy. It seemed as if the sky were going to break and fall on the earth. I was furious and afraid, and so were my friends.[28]

Beah practiced stabbing a banana tree with a bayonet, urged by his commander to think of it as a rebel who had murdered his family. At home Beah had been an avid reader, and he often traded quotes from Shakespeare with the lieutenant. It was the last vestige of civilization in his life at the camp.

Drills eventually gave way to actual fighting. Beah and the other soldiers would raid rebel camps and loot the houses of villagers who supported the insurgents. Following one raid, he was ordered to assist in killing several prisoners. His lieutenant made a game of the executions, rewarding the soldier whose prisoner died first. Beah was declared the winner. He admits that he was able to slice his prisoner's throat without emotion. For the next two years, his time was split between relaxing with fellow soldiers—which meant watching movies,

Recruited for Suicide

In the summer of 2015 militants with ISIS staged a series of raids on villages in Anbar Province, west of Baghdad in Iraq. The militants kidnapped as many as four hundred children in Anbar, presumably with the intention of training them as fighters. About one hundred more youths were seized in Diyali Province in the east. Authorities in Iraq suspect that the children were transported to bases in Iraq and Syria for training. The fear is that many of the children are being brainwashed to serve as suicide bombers.

ISIS militants have employed children for suicide missions before, but use of the tactic seems to be increasing. Children are brainwashed to believe their holy duty is to carry out suicide bombings against their enemies. Often they are drugged before embarking on their suicide missions. Considered expendable while alive, they are praised as martyrs after death and held up as examples of supreme courage and sacrifice to other young soldiers. In July 2015 ISIS rebels strapped fourteen-year-old Mar Hadid Al-Muhammad behind the wheel of a truck filled with explosives. The boy rammed the truck into a Kurdish checkpoint near the Syrian city of Hasakah. The explosion killed fifty Kurdish soldiers. ISIS immediately posted on social media pictures of the boy taken moments before he sped off on his suicide mission. Mar Hadid is shown wide-eyed with apprehension, his index finger pointing upward in the ISIS salute.

smoking marijuana, and sniffing cocaine—and going on raids. He became hardened to the life of a soldier:

> The villages that we captured and turned into our bases as we went along and the forests that we slept in became my home. My squad was my family, my gun was my provider and protector, and my rule was to kill or be killed. The extent of my thoughts didn't go much beyond that. We had been fighting for over two years, and killing had become a daily activity. I felt no pity for anyone. My childhood had gone by without my knowing, and it seemed as if my heart had frozen.[29]

Beah's career as a child soldier came to a sudden end. One day a truck arrived with four men in white T-shirts that said UNICEF in large blue letters. Pressure from the UN led the lieutenant to hand over Beah and his youngest companions as illegal child soldiers. They were transported to a fenced compound, where they were held—unwisely—with youths who had fought on the rebel side. Even separated from the war, Beah and his comrades fought the rebel boys with fists and bayonets. When guards tried to break up the fight, boys from both sides overwhelmed them and snatched their guns. Six boys were killed before more guards arrived to stop the fighting. It would take years of therapy to quell Beah's instinct for violence.

A War of Madness

As suggested by Ishmael Beah's experience, drugs often play a large part in driving child soldiers to frenzied violence. Conflicts that begin as a principled uprising against a corrupt government often degenerate into an endless series of raids and opportunities for looting. And the looting pays for drugs. "There might have been a little rhetoric at the beginning," says Beah. "But very quickly the ideology gets lost. And then it just becomes a bloodbath, a way for the commanders to plunder, a war of madness."[30] Commanders make sure that drugs are plentiful and their soldiers—particularly the youngest ones—are kept high. This not only lowers their inhibitions and induces fearlessness in battle, it also makes them dependent on the drugs and thus easier to control. To help secure their loyalty, soldiers are also awarded young female captives as child brides or sex slaves. The *New York Times* described Joseph Kony's LRA in Uganda as "a drugged-out street gang living in the jungle with military-grade weaponry and 13-year-old brides."[31]

The life of a child soldier unfolds in the shadows. Commanders exploit them as replaceable parts, with no regard for their survival. Child soldiers are forced to lead assaults and take risks older fighters avoid. Torn from their homes and families, child soldiers lose all the benefits of civilization, learning to kill without remorse. Many become addicted to a life of violence fueled by drugs. Often their only hope is that some outside group such as UNICEF will somehow intervene to demand their freedom and get them the help they desperately need. Otherwise the likely fate for a child soldier is an early death.

"We had been fighting for over two years, and killing had become a daily activity. I felt no pity for anyone. My childhood had gone by without my knowing, and it seemed as if my heart had frozen."[29]

—Ishmael Beah, a former child soldier in Sierra Leone.

Chapter 4

Returning to Civilian Life

Of thousands of children caught up as fighters in South Sudan's civil war, Emmanuel Jal is one of the few lucky ones. Jal was recruited at age eight, after witnessing the rape of his aunt and torching of his home village by Sudanese rebels. He relished the opportunity to avenge these crimes with AK-47 in hand. In the late 1980s Jal became embroiled in a violent way of life. He saw unspeakable horrors, watched hundreds of young comrades meet bloody ends, and committed brutal acts himself. Somehow, against all odds, he not only survived but found his way to freedom. Around 1992 British aid worker Emma McCune met Jal at his lowest ebb, returning from a lengthy battle half starved while his fellow soldiers resorted to cannibalism to survive. McCune managed to smuggle Jal to Kenya aboard a British plane. There she saw that he was clothed, fed, and enrolled in school. Jal thought of her as his guardian angel, having rescued him from a hopeless situation in South Sudan. Inspired by McCune (who died in a car crash months after saving Jal), he moved to London in 2005 and wrote a book about his harrowing years as a child soldier. Working on the book dredged up terrible nightmares about Jal's former life, but he knew it was important to tell the truth. A talented hip-hop musician, actor, and writer, Jal has used his story to draw attention to the plight of child soldiers the world over. "Yeah, I used to have a lot of nightmares—life was difficult then," he says. "But music became the place [where] I was able to see heaven. So through music I was able to dance, I was able to become a child again."[32]

A Struggle to Reintegrate into Society

Success stories for former child soldiers like Jal are rare. Young people who survive face all sorts of physical, social, and emotional problems. Almost everything about their experience as a child soldier increases the difficulty of reintegrating into normal society. Many child soldiers bear physical wounds and injuries from fighting. These include gunshot wounds, stabbings, broken bones, and blunt force injuries—the latter often the result of their commanders' brutal discipline. Due to lack of proper medical care and unhygienic places for treatment, wounds can worsen into permanent disabilities. Child soldiers often suffer from other health problems, ranging from drug addiction to cholera, HIV/AIDS, and malnutrition. Dr. Robin Nandy, senior health adviser for emergencies at UNICEF's Health Section in New York, says:

> When one thinks of health needs in a conflict situation— and this applies to children and adults—there is a tendency to think of war injuries. But it's important to recognize the threat posed by psychosocial trauma and common diseases in crisis situations—diseases like malaria, cholera and yellow fever, exposure to which results from the breakdown of social systems and increased vulnerability that occur in conflicts, especially when they are prolonged. A child that gets sick in a war zone does not get the treatment he or she might otherwise receive.[33]

Establishing some kind of normal life can seem almost impossible to a former child soldier. Returning youths generally find themselves in a ramshackle society roiled by civil war and struggling to provide the most basic infrastructure for its citizens. Wandering on their own, some return to their old villages but find no family or friends to help them. Those who try their luck in the cities rarely can find work. Most are illiterate, have no identification cards or papers, and have grown accustomed to getting what they need by force. In warfare child soldiers care only about surviving the day, living instinctively from moment to moment with no thought of the future, a habit of mind that does not bode well for success in ordinary society.

The most fortunate child soldiers gain release from their units through international groups such as UNICEF, the World Health Organization, and other nongovernmental organizations (NGOs).

Emmanuel Jal (pictured in London in 2015) escaped the brutality of his life as a child soldier in South Sudan. He was recruited at age eight after watching the rape of his aunt and the destruction of his home village.

Officials from these groups can help return the youths to school or get them into vocational training programs that teach skills such as carpentry and computer literacy. Those who escape on their own or are abandoned by their comrades face a tougher task reintegrating into society. Many are shunned by civilians, who suspect them of being killers and rapists. Villagers who themselves are struggling to get by have little sympathy to spare for former soldiers, even children, who are perceived as the source of their misery. The result for released child soldiers is more anger, guilt, and feelings of worthlessness. "These children have often lost their families and so have no network of support, no way to make a living," says Obonyo Tom Fred, director of a community association in northern Uganda. "It is so hard for them. I have heard some say they were better off in the war zone."[34]

Dealing with Post-Traumatic Stress Disorder

For returning child soldiers, illness, injuries, and lack of education can pale next to the emotional stress of what they have undergone. All too typical is the case of a boy abducted by Joseph Kony's LRA at age seven. To prove his loyalty, he was forced to kill his uncle with a machete. For years he roamed with Kony's forces, witnessing daily atrocities and forced to commit terrible acts himself. At age fourteen he escaped back to his home village in northern Uganda. His parents' joy at his return fell away when they realized how much their son had changed. The boy could not sleep at night. Some days he would suddenly run screaming through the village. He struggled with thoughts of suicide. "No one knew what to do with him," says Peter Oketayot, a mental health counselor who treated the boy. "They were calling him names. They thought he was mad, or crazy."[35] Oketayot found that the boy was suffering from depression and post-traumatic stress disorder (PTSD). People with PTSD have usually survived some terrifying ordeal and continue to feel stressed or frightened even though the original danger has passed.

Children like Oketayot's patient who have been exposed to violence over a long period typically show evidence of PTSD and depression. Studies of former child soldiers in the African nation of Liberia revealed that 90 percent had symptoms of PTSD and 65 percent showed signs of major depression. Many former child soldiers suffer from insomnia and persistent thoughts of suicide. Along with these problems, child soldiers often lack a moral compass and any feelings of a social bond. Constant involvement in violent acts has made them insensitive to violence and unable to judge between right and wrong. They frequently seek excitement and

"These children have often lost their families and so have no network of support, no way to make a living. . . . I have heard some say they were better off in the war zone."[34]

—Obonyo Tom Fred, director of a community association in northern Uganda.

Building Schools in South Sudan

One major problem faced by former child soldiers in trying to resume a normal life is their lack of education. Many have lost years of schooling and fallen far behind students of their age. The ravages of war often have left schools in their home villages unusable. Makeshift grass huts frequently must serve as classrooms. In some areas of South Sudan, a new nation that has been hobbled by poverty and civil war, only one in ten children has attended a primary school, and large numbers of adults cannot read. To address the problem of education in South Sudan, a group called Mothering Across Continents is soliciting donations worldwide. The project, called Raising South Sudan, is the brainchild of two former Sudanese child soldiers, Ngor Kur Mayol and James Lubo Mijak. Mayol and Mijak are part of the so-called Lost Boys of Sudan—refugees and child soldiers who traveled to the United States in 2001 to become citizens and get an education. The two hope to share their good fortune with their compatriots by building permanent schools in South Sudan.

Donations pay for basics such as books, student uniforms, and teacher salaries. The funds also help build and furnish new classrooms as well as provide bathroom facilities and clean water. In 2013 Raising South Sudan opened its first permanent primary school in Mijak's home village of Nyarweng. More recently the group has built an orphanage and school called *Gumriak,* which translates as "those who survived the disaster."

Quoted in Mothering Across Continents, "Raising South Sudan," 2014. www.motheringacrosscontinents.org.

display aggressive behavior toward others. Lingering drug addiction can compound their difficulties.

Experts believe that reintegrating child soldiers into society requires a stronger focus on mental health counseling. Nina Winkler, a psychologist at the University of Konstanz in Germany, says studies indicate that child soldiers with PTSD benefit most from talking through their problems with trained psychiatric counselors. She believes school-based mental health programs might be effective for treatment. Yet war-torn areas that produce scores of child soldiers tend to have few hospitals or mental health clinics and little money for building them. Winkler frankly admits that financing is a problem.

Challenges Faced by Girls Who Return

Mental health is key to reintegration for child soldiers of both sexes. Research shows that girls who have been abducted by

A former child soldier from Uganda bears the lasting physical scars of war. He was shot—and then left for dead—by a Lord's Resistance Army commander for not carrying enough supplies.

Misconceptions About Rehabilitating Child Soldiers

Since returning to ordinary life, former child soldier Ishmael Beah has achieved great success. Moving to the United States, he earned a degree in political science from Oberlin College in 2004. Since then he has published two books and traveled the world speaking about the plight of child soldiers. Here, in an excerpt from an interview with NPR, Beah explains certain misconceptions about rehabilitating child soldiers.

How do you move into the future while the past is still trying to pull at you very strongly?

What do you do with a certain skill set and certain habits and certain things that you've acquired during war? Sometimes some of these things don't need to be washed out of you, as most people will think. Whenever they see a former child soldier, they will think, "Oh, you need complete rehabilitation. You need to forget everything that happened in order to have a life." No, sometimes you don't. . . .

Survival requires a remarkable intelligence. Also being able to know that when one is selfish, what it does to society. When one wants everything for themselves—knowing that and not wanting that to repeat itself. Also knowing how to resist people trampling all over you as a human being and dehumanizing you. Some of these things can be used for positive force. Some of the things that young people learn during war—even though I don't want anybody to go to war—can be refocused in a positive way.

Quoted in Renee Montagne, "A Former Child Soldier Imagines 'Tomorrow' in Sierra Leone," NPR, January 9, 2014. www.npr.org.

armed groups face higher rates of psychological distress than boys. They tend to be more vulnerable to PTSD and depression, not only from the fighting they have lived through but from the traumas of rape and sexual abuse they have suffered. Girls who return from serving in militias bear the marks of their brutal treatment, both as soldiers and sex slaves. Their plight in captivity has been mainly hidden from view, brushed aside by militia leaders who refer to the young females as wives or sisters. Many girls in armed groups have given birth practically on the battlefield or suffered painful miscarriages or forcible abortions. Upon their return home, they often are stigmatized for having collaborated with marauding rebels—despite the fact they were abducted at gunpoint and forced into a kind of slavery.

One Ugandan woman recalls being kidnapped from her parents' home when she was only nine years old. Rebels made her endure long marches and learn to operate large guns, and they took her on raids during which many atrocities were committed. Brainwashed to obey, she would kill without mercy. She was regularly beaten and tortured—and at one point forced to sit on a pile of dead bodies and commune with their spirits—and she was sexually assaulted countless times. At age thirteen she finally escaped. "When I returned home," she says, "many people did not accept me. They would disturb me all the time, yelling horrible things to me. I think they were afraid of me because of what I had done before. They didn't understand that it wasn't really me then."[36] At first she was tormented by nightmares and terrible memories of those violent days with the rebels. With her parents unable to afford her school fees, she soon drifted into living with an older man. At fourteen, it seemed she was destined for further abuse and exploitation. However, social workers in Uganda reached out to the girl. They helped her enter a vocational school, where she learned bakery skills and the rudiments of business. Today she is married with two children and hopes to start her own bakery one day.

"When I returned home, many people did not accept me. . . . I think they were afraid of me because of what I had done before. They didn't understand that it wasn't really me then."[36]

—A Ugandan woman who was kidnapped by rebels at age nine.

Some girls who have escaped from armed groups help other former child soldiers in their efforts to rejoin society. Adriana was twelve years old—three days shy of graduating from fifth grade—when she followed her older siblings' example and joined the Marxist National Liberation Army, the largest of several guerrilla groups in Colombia's brutal long-term civil war. Over six years she rose to become second in command of a unit with three hundred men. Captured by government soldiers the day before her eighteenth birthday, Adriana was sent to a transitional home, the first step in the government's rehabilitation program for child soldiers. At first Adriana rebelled against the teachers, psychologists, and other staff at the home. She hoped her bad behavior would gain her release back to the guerrillas in the field. Eventually, however, she found an interest in books. She identified with the shoeshine-boy hero of one novel who rose from poverty to success in business. She began to apply the discipline she had acquired in the guerrilla camp to her activities at the school. A class in hairstyling led to a job at a salon. Soon she joined a five-person team with Mercy Corps in Colombia, seeking to use her experience to help other former guerrilla fighters like herself reintegrate into society. Females who have managed to break away from the armed groups respond to her honesty and treat her as a confidant. "I feel very happy to be able to help the young people because I belonged to them," says Adriana. "When they come here, they don't have self-confidence; we don't know what it is to trust another person. . . . It's so gratifying when the young people come to you and say, 'Thank you for teaching me, thank you for listening to me.'"[37]

Rejecting the Path to Normalcy

Education and mental health treatment are a vital part of the rehabilitation process for former child soldiers. But some child soldiers instinctively rebel against any attempt to return them to normal life. Ishmael Beah had to overcome these feelings after military police delivered him and his comrades to Benin House, a rehabilitation center on the outskirts of Freetown in Sierra Leone. At first Beah felt nothing but contempt for the nurses and staff members who were trying to help him. At the end of each meal, when social workers would urge him and the other former child combatants to undergo regular medical checkups or attend one-on-one counseling sessions, the boys would throw food, bowls, spoons, and even benches at them. Frustrated at being confined, Beah and his friends would fight among themselves, randomly attack kitchen workers, or throw stones at neighbors walking near the facility. Beah hated the security personnel at the facility, who, in their clean uniforms, represented to him the city police who knew nothing of real combat. Yet through it all the workers at Benin House remained stubbornly supportive. One staff member, an ex-military man called Poppay, was stabbed in the foot by one of the boys and then beaten by a group that included Beah. He met the boys several days later with a limp and a smile. Poppay's willingness to forgive was infuriating, Beah recalls:

> "It is not your fault that you did such a thing to me," he said, as he strolled through the dining hall. This made us angry, because we wanted "the civilians," as we referred to the staff members, to respect us as soldiers who were capable of severely harming them. Most of the staff members were

53

like that; they returned smiling after we hurt them. It was as if they had made a pact not to give up on us. Their smiles made us hate them all the more.[38]

Shortly thereafter, Beah broke out the windows of his assigned classroom with his bare fist. He sullenly refused to speak to the nurse who bandaged his hand. She offered him a glass of water, but he smashed it against the clinic wall. When Beah and the other boys were given school supplies—books, pens, and pencils—they repeatedly used them to build campfires. Like other child soldiers, Beah suffered from nightmares and migraines, tormented by violent images. "I would dream that a faceless gunman had tied me up and begun to slit my throat with the zigzag edge of his bayonet,"[39] he recalls. He would turn on the faucet and imagine that it produced gushes of blood. He often would awake screaming, sweating, and throwing punches in the middle of the night.

> "I would dream that a faceless gunman had tied me up and begun to slit my throat with the zigzag edge of his bayonet."[39]
>
> —Ishmael Beah, a former child soldier in Sierra Leone.

Eventually, however, he began to respond to the staff at Benin House, to their civilizing influence. Esther, the nurse who had tended to Beah, became a trusted friend. Several months after arriving at the facility, Beah was able to rejoin society and live with his uncle. Visiting officials from UNICEF approached him about traveling to New York City, where he could deliver his account of life as a child soldier. He saw Esther only one more time. "She was wearing her white uniform and was on her way to take on other traumatized children," Beah remembers. "It must be tough living with so many war stories. I was just living with one, mine, and it was difficult. . . . Why does she do it? Why do they all do it?"[40] Beah, like other child soldiers who have managed to escape their past, owes much to dedicated people like Esther, who refused to give up on him. He calls the opportunity they gave him "this second lifetime of mine."[41]

Chapter 5

Addressing the Problem of Child Soldiers

The Acholi people of northern Uganda have seen thousands of their children suffer abduction and subsequent lives as child soldiers or sex slaves. Rather than heaping blame on these young people for committing violent acts or collaborating with Joseph Kony's LRA rebels, the Acholi seek reconciliation in order to achieve peace and heal their community. One traditional ceremony of atonement is called *Mato Oput*, which means "drinking the bitter root." Returning child soldiers accept responsibility for their actions and ask for forgiveness from victims' families. Some offer to pay reparations. They share a drink of the bitter root mixture from a calabash, or gourd, to overcome the bitterness of soured relations. Mato Oput is often accompanied by other cleansing rituals, such as walking on eggs before entering a home or bending spears to symbolize an end to hostilities. The Acholi believe the Mato Oput ceremony is more effective than harsh retribution in helping former child soldiers reconcile their guilt and go back to normal life. Like many social workers and mental health professionals, Ugandans are focused on practical ways to address the growing problem of child soldiers.

Offering Support with Talk Therapy

In northern Uganda psychiatric workers reinforce Mato Oput with a counseling technique called narrative exposure therapy (NET). Former child soldiers are urged to talk about all the things that happened to them under Kony's control and the terrible things they were forced to do. Thus, NET can be an effective approach for children struggling with symptoms of PTSD. Typically, young victims cannot produce a coherent narrative of a traumatic event, due to the emotional stress produced by certain memories. The use of storytelling with NET enables the victims to confront the reality of past events and realize their reactions to them are normal. They are able to remove the emotional response and change so-called hot memories that trigger traumatic reactions to cold memories that are much less stressful. "By allowing these child soldiers to detail their story," mental health researchers Tara Shertel and Joanne Sills explain, "they begin to realize that what happened in the past is not entirely their fault; they begin to forgive themselves, which allows the community to also forgive. NET serves as a transition state for these victims to slowly assimilate back into the community."[42]

Peter Oketayot is a counselor in northern Uganda trained to use NET with former child soldiers. One of Oketayot's teenage patients became suicidal and had recurrent nightmares. The boy's screams in the darkness were interpreted by some villagers as proof he was going mad from guilt. Oketayot encouraged the boy to tell his painful stories in detail. "Sometimes during the counseling sessions he would begin to relive the event," says Oketayot. "You could see the reaction in his body. We had to call him back, we would shout his name and use very strong smelling jellies to pull him back."[43] Yet after a few weeks, the youth began to improve. Oketayot followed up after four months and again after nine months. The former child soldier showed definite signs of healing. "He even told us, 'I feel better. I feel like myself again,'" Oketayot says. "As a counselor, that's what makes me happy."[44]

Although many Ugandans believe their methods of reconciliation are helping end the conflict with Kony's LRA, others continue to pursue more traditional justice. In January 2016 the International Criminal Court in The Hague began criminal proceedings against Dominic Ongwen for war crimes he committed as one of Kony's commanders. Ongwen has led a life of extreme violence in the forests of Uganda, mutilating victims of his raids and ordering child soldiers under his command to beat to death other children caught trying to escape. Yet Ongwen's defenders point out that he was only ten years old when LRA soldiers abducted him on his way home from school. He had little choice but to follow Kony's orders, they say. "He had to either follow those rules and survive, or frankly, die," explains Ledio Cakaj, an independent consultant who has studied Kony's LRA for almost a decade. "So to a certain extent we are holding him responsible for being alive. Particularly if you understand the story of people who are not here anymore because they either refused or were unable to perform the same way that Ongwen did."[45] Ongwen's controversial case highlights the difficulty of separating the actor from the act when dealing with war crimes among former child soldiers. Most observers are

Indicted for war crimes, Dominic Ongwen (right) appears at the International Criminal Court in The Hague in 2015. Forced to join the Lord's Resistance Army at age ten, he rose to become a commander who was known for his extreme brutality.

more comfortable supporting the prosecution of individuals like Congolese warlord Thomas Lubanga Dyilo. Lubanga regularly recruited and employed in combat children under the age of fifteen.

Programs to Help Child Soldiers

International sanctions against those who recruit child soldiers do little to help the children themselves rejoin society and lead a normal life. For this, government officials and aid groups have employed programs with a three-pronged approach: disarmament, demobilization, and reintegration (DDR). These DDR programs have met with some success in war-torn nations such as Liberia, Sierra Leone, and South Sudan. The goal is to set up a peace process that makes the society more stable and enables combatants, including child soldiers, to get the assistance they need. Disarmament removes weapons from the hands of fighters and often from civilians as well. Demobilization obtains the release of fighters from armed groups. Reintegration—the key step—seeks to return ex-combatants to society with jobs and sustainable income. UN peacekeeping officials are trained to focus on protecting and aiding children in DDR programs. Specially trained workers, called child protection advisers, coordinate with UN Police, military officials, and local government representatives to protect and offer aid to former child soldiers and other abductees. In Liberia, DDR efforts saw a number of NGO partners working together, including UNICEF, the World Food Program, the World Health Organization, ActionAid, and the United Nations Development Programme.

One of the most thorough test cases to date of the DDR approach took place in Sierra Leone in 2001–2002. This followed two failed attempts at DDR in that nation, the last in 2000, until British military intervention finally brought an end to years of civil war. The cease-fire enabled officials to pursue the DDR process in a somewhat orderly fashion, albeit with occasional eruptions of more fighting. UNICEF and various child-focused NGOs agreed to separate the DDR for children from that for adults and also to tailor the DDR program to the different needs of boys

Sister Rosemary Nyirumbe

In the quest to help former child soldiers and abductees adjust to civilian life, the personal touch can make all the difference. Sister Rosemary Nyirumbe, a resolute Ugandan nun based in Gulu, has helped more than two thousand girls who have fled captivity in the LRA of Kony. The girls have been doubly traumatized from being trained as fighters and exploited as sex slaves by rebel commanders. Many of them return with babies fathered by their captors, which leaves the girls feeling insecure and in fear of rejection by their families and neighbors. With this in mind, Sister Rosemary has created a safe haven for the girls called Saint Monica's Girls Tailoring Centre, a place that feels more like a home than an institution. In radio announcements, Sister Rosemary emphasizes that every girl is welcome. "I said that I would like you to come here in the situation you are," she explains. "If you are a mother, come with your child. If you are pregnant come as you are and even if you are raped, come as you are."

At Saint Monica's the girls learn sewing and dressmaking skills and also develop a sense of self-worth. Sister Rosemary compares sewing pieces of cloth into garments with the work of mending a broken spirit. She hopes someday to provide long-term education for her girls. "I am a dreamer and having a dream is sometimes challenging," says Sister Rosemary, "but I never look at a situation as too difficult."

Quoted in Purvi Thacker, "'I Am a Dreamer,' Says the Ugandan Nun Saving Scores of Girls Kidnapped by Warlord Joseph Kony," Women in the World and *New York Times*, April 23, 2015. http://nytlive.nytimes .com.

and girls. Between May 2001 and January 2002, 4,674 young people were demobilized in Sierra Leone. This was in addition to the more than 2,000 others whose release had been negotiated by the UN and other groups since 1998.

Demobilized young people were separated from adult soldiers and commanders in order to break the links of control. Most children entered an Interim Care Center (ICC) managed by one of the NGOs dedicated to child protection. The young people received health care for themselves and, when needed, for their

Two young women, ages sixteen and eighteen, join other teens in learning how to use a sewing machine at a rehabilitation center for former child soldiers in Uganda. Centers like this one teach job skills to former youth combatants.

infants. Workers at the ICC began the process of locating parents or relatives. They also set up a regular schedule of classes, art and music activities, and chores to instill in the youths a sense of order and community. Former child soldiers particularly valued school classes and skills training, both of which improved their job prospects.

Results of DDR in Sierra Leone were mixed. On the positive side, 98 percent of the demobilized child soldiers and other captive children were able to reunite with one or both parents or with relatives. Mental health workers helped ease the children's return to the community by encouraging forgiveness and reconciliation among families and neighbors. As John Williamson of the US Agency for International Development notes:

> In contrast to earlier hostility toward the return of former
> RUF child soldiers, during my visit to Sierra Leone in 2002,

community members spoke eloquently about their forgiveness for these children because they understood that they had been forced to do what they did. . . . The real heroes of the process, the ones who have been on the front line and made it work, have been the Sierra Leonean staff, community leaders, grass-roots volunteers, and resilient children.[46]

Williamson found that former child soldiers who had gone through traditional cleansing ceremonies and had received follow-up visits from NGO personnel measured higher in social acceptance, well-being, and freedom from PTSD.

Some of the main problems with DDR involved disarmament. Too often peacekeepers assumed that once a child soldier was relieved of his or her weapon, the rest of the process would be easy. Many child soldiers demanded the same treatment as adult combatants, who had received cash payments for their weapons. Some tried to keep their guns as a means of getting food or money if necessary. Peacekeepers also confused the guidelines regarding weapons. They would offer assistance only to those children deemed to be former soldiers because they had a weapon to turn in. Because of this, peacekeepers overlooked many children who had helped the militias by performing tasks other than fighting. This included girls who had been sexually enslaved or exploited. In fact, the neglect of these so-called lost girls was a major failing of DDR. "Some girls were not allowed by their commanders, or 'bush husbands,' to go through DDR," says Williamson. "Many kept themselves out of the process out of fear or shame."[47]

"The real heroes of the process, the ones who have been on the front line and made it work, have been the Sierra Leonean staff, community leaders, grass-roots volunteers, and resilient children."[46]

—John Williamson, an official with the US Agency for International Development.

The Need for Ongoing Care

In Sierra Leone, as in other war-ravaged areas, assistance rapidly faded once the headline-grabbing conflict ended. Today Sierra Leone ranks near the bottom worldwide in the UN Human Development Index. Many former child soldiers there struggle without jobs and health care. Mental health services are especially lacking—the nation's lone psychiatrist is soon to retire. All too often, once the killing has subsided and peace treaties are signed, the emergency personnel disappear, leaving behind a population in desperate need. Theresa Betancourt, director of Harvard University's Research Program on Children and Global Adversity, says vulnerable former child soldiers deserve better. "We need to devise lasting systems of care," says Betancourt, "instead of leaving behind a dust cloud that disappears when the humanitarian actors leave."[48]

Betancourt first traveled to Sierra Leone in 2002, as the bloody eleven-year civil war was winding down. She talked to child soldiers and was shocked by how young they looked, their tattered uniforms hanging on malnourished frames. She was inspired to conduct a systematic study of the boys' and girls' postwar experiences—the feelings of guilt and shame, the social isolation, the problems with anxiety and addiction. Her research has convinced her that effective treatments, and clinical trials to measure them, can be done in poor rural communities wracked by war. Like other experts, Betancourt believes the answer lies with practical mental health interventions for former child soldiers. The goal should be to forge stronger connections to family and community. Struggling young people can gain confidence and a sense of purpose by returning to school or entering job training programs. Above all, the children should continue to discuss what they went through—with therapists, with family and friends, and with each other. "The key is being able to put a word to their feelings: sadness, worthlessness, hopelessness, loss of energy, the sense that life is not worth living," says

"Once intervention and problem solving begins, these young people no longer feel alone. Their symptoms start to lift."[49]

—Theresa Betancourt, director of Harvard University's Research Program on Children and Global Adversity.

Prosecuting Recruiters in Colombia

The politics of cease-fire negotiations can derail efforts to prosecute those who recruit child soldiers. In September 2015 a Colombian judge sentenced two leaders of the rebel group FARC to thirteen years in prison for recruiting children into a guerrilla unit. The rebel leaders—one known as Timochenko and the other as Iván Márquez—were sentenced in absentia, meaning they were not in the court's custody. During the hearing, prosecutors showed that of sixty-three guerrillas killed in combat with Colombia's military between November 2000 and March 2001, twenty-five were minors. Among these dead children were nine girls fitted with intrauterine devices, which the medical examiner saw as proof of their sexual abuse by FARC leaders. Yet Timochenko and Márquez almost certainly will escape punishment. Critics say that Colombian president Juan Manuel Santos is so anxious to secure a peace deal with the FARC that he is willing to pardon these offenses against children as lesser political crimes, similar to drug dealing or extortion.

The Colombian Institute for Family Welfare estimates that the FARC still has more than two thousand children and adolescents in its ranks. During peace talks, FARC leaders claimed they do not use children younger than seventeen, but shortly thereafter they discharged more than a dozen children under age fifteen. American journalist Lia Fowler contends the government does not want these figures known. "[The children's] numbers and the graphic details of what they've been through would ignite public outrage against the FARC and any amnesty proposal," says Fowler.

Quoted in Mary Anastasia O'Grady, "Do Colombian Children Matter?," *Wall Street Journal*, October 25, 2015. www.wsj.com.

Betancourt. "We spend a lot of time trying to learn local terms for emotional suffering. Once intervention and problem solving begins, these young people no longer feel alone. Their symptoms start to lift."[49] Betancourt calls her program the Youth Readiness Intervention because it helps prepare former child soldiers for success in life, free from the horrors of war.

The Struggle to End the Use of Child Soldiers

No one has yet devised a practical way of ending the recruitment and exploitation of child soldiers. Governments worldwide regularly sign agreements and express support for programs to end the practice. With the best intentions, activists solicit donations and work to raise awareness about the abuse of child soldiers. Yet wherever conflicts erupt, children are still sent into battle in depressingly large numbers. One of the most comprehensive reports on the problem ever compiled, the Child

Soldiers Global Report 2008, declared that "despite the best efforts of UN agencies, NGOs and others, large-scale releases of children from armed forces or groups have rarely taken place before hostilities end. . . . Indeed, where armed conflict does exist, child soldiers will almost certainly be involved."[50] Seemingly the only way to stop the use of child soldiers is to prevent war from occurring—an outcome that history suggests is highly unlikely.

Nonetheless, several worldwide groups have useful programs to help prevent the recruitment of child soldiers. These include Amnesty International, International Rescue Committee, and Invisible Children. For example, Invisible Children, which operates in Central Africa, maintains an Early Warning Radio Network to warn villagers in the region of impending attacks by Kony's LRA rebels. These warnings can enable families to hide their children or take steps to protect them. Invisible Children also makes broadcasts and distributes fliers that encourage rebel soldiers—many of whom are weak from illness or exhaustion—to stop fighting, release young abductees, and return home. It has set up Community Defection Committees to motivate villagers to accept rebel defectors who might themselves have been abducted as children.

Amnesty International and other human rights organizations constantly monitor the use of child soldiers and publicly expose nations or leaders who allow the practice to continue. In this regard, Western nations can also play a major role. In the United States, the 2008 Child Soldier Prevention Act requires the secretary of state to publish an annual report listing governments that recruit and use child soldiers or that support armed groups that employ child soldiers. Countries that make the list are subject to restrictions on military aid and equipment. Although in practice some of these countries receive waivers that allow military aid to continue, the act has had success in getting other foreign governments to sign action plans and to begin reducing the number of child soldiers within their borders. Concrete results like this prove that political pressure can make a difference.

The Future for Child Soldiers

Despite attempts to publicize the problem of child soldiers, too often these children remain in the shadows, their plight almost forgotten in the larger chaos of warfare. It is up to ordinary citizens the world over to keep raising this issue with their leaders and to support the efforts of NGOs dedicated to ending the recruitment of child soldiers. These captive children must rely on others to demand that they be freed. Roméo Dallaire, who led UN peace-keeping forces in the 1994 Rwandan genocide, says to those wondering how to help, "I will not rest from my goal of eradicating the use of child soldiers. I ask you to join me on this mission. The humanity of these children is as real and valid as your own, and I know you will not fail them. . . . The time is now and the moment is yours to grasp."[51]

Source Notes

Introduction: Sold into Service

1. Quoted in Spike Johnson, "The Hard Life of Burma's Child Soldiers," Pulitzer Center on Crisis Reporting, April 9, 2015. http://pulitzercenter.org.
2. Quoted in Johnson, "The Hard Life of Burma's Child Soldiers."
3. Quoted in Siddharth Chatterjee, "For Child Soldiers, Every Day Is a Living Nightmare," *Forbes*, December 9, 2012. www.forbes.com.

Chapter 1: The Problem of Child Soldiers Today

4. Quoted in Human Rights Watch, "Maybe We Live and Maybe We Die," June 22, 2014. www.hrw.org.
5. Jo Becker, "Dispatches: Obama Still Arms Governments Using Child Soldiers," Human Rights Watch, October 1, 2015. www.hrw.org.
6. UNICEF, "Factsheet: Child Soldiers." www.unicef.org.
7. War Child, "Child Soldiers." www.warchild.org.
8. Andrew Friedman, "Child Soldiers in Africa: A Problem That Won't Just Go Away," AFK Insider, September 11, 2014. http://afkinsider.com.
9. Quoted in Amnesty International, "A Compromised Future: Children Recruited by Armed Forces and Groups in Eastern Chad," ReliefWeb, February 10, 2011. http://reliefweb.int/report.
10. Quoted in Amnesty International, "A Compromised Future."
11. Quoted in Amy S. Choi, "Nearly Half of Child Soldiers Are Girls," *Salon*, February 21, 2013. www.salon.com.
12. Quoted in Isabelle de Grave, "Former Girl Soldiers Trade One Nightmare for Another," Inter Press Service News Agency, June 14, 2012. www.ipsnews.net.

13. Roméo Dallaire, *They Fight like Soldiers, They Die Like Children: The Global Quest to Eradicate the Use of Child Soldiers*. New York: Walker, 2010, p. 4.

Chapter 2: Recruiting Children to Fight

14. Quoted in Human Rights Watch, "Maybe We Live and Maybe We Die."
15. Quoted in Philip Obaji Jr., "The Child Soldiers Fighting Boko Haram," *Daily Beast*, March 7, 2015. www.thedailybeast.com.
16. Quoted in Obaji, "The Child Soldiers Fighting Boko Haram."
17. Jeffrey Gettleman, "Africa's Forever Wars: Why the Continent's Conflicts Never End," *Foreign Policy*, February 11, 2010. http://foreignpolicy.com.
18. Quoted in Will Storr, "Kony's Child Soldiers: 'When You Kill for the First Time, You Change,'" *Telegraph* (London), February 12, 2014. www.telegraph.co.uk.
19. Quoted in Storr, "Kony's Child Soldiers."
20. Quoted in Lizzie Dearden, "Hundreds of Boys 'Kidnapped' and Forced into Becoming Child Soldiers in South Sudan," *Independent* (London), March 1, 2015. www.independent.co.uk.
21. Quoted in Human Rights Watch, "South Sudan: Government Forces Recruiting Child Soldiers," February 16, 2015. www.hrw.org.
22. Quoted in Nick Dorman, "ISIS Using Child Soldiers in Slick and Sick Video to Lure Young British Recruits," *Mirror Online*, June 20, 2015. www.mirror.co.uk.

Chapter 3: Life of a Child Soldier

23. Quoted in Francesca Trianni, "Watch: Syrian Children Talk About Life as Child Soldiers," *Time*, June 22, 2014. http://time.com.
24. Quoted in Taylor Luck, "As Syrian Rebels' Losses Mount, Teenagers Begin Filling Ranks," *Washington Post*, August 24, 2013. www.washingtonpost.com.

25. Quoted in Ann O'Neill, "Stolen Kids Turned into Terrifying Killers," CNN, February 12, 2007. www.cnn.com.
26. Jeff Koinange, "Koinange: Friend Gunned Down by Child Soldiers," CNN, February 12, 2007. www.cnn.com.
27. Quoted in Rita Rosenfeld, "Junior Atrocities," *Politic?* (blog), July 21, 2015. http://rita-rosenfeld.blogspot.com.
28. Ishmael Beah, *A Long Way Gone: Memoirs of a Boy Soldier*. New York: Crichton, 2007, p. 108.
29. Beah, *A Long Way Gone*, p. 126.
30. Quoted in Dallaire, *They Fight like Soldiers, They Die Like Children*, p. 115.
31. Jeffrey Gettleman, "The Perfect Weapon for the Meanest Wars," *New York Times*, April 29, 2007. www.nytimes.com.

Chapter 4: Returning to Civilian Life

32. Quoted in Scott Simon, "A Former Child Soldier Finds Escape, Heaven Through His Music," interview, NPR, January 31, 2015. www.npr.org.
33. Quoted in World Health Organization, "Healing Child Soldiers," *Bulletin of the World Health Organization*, May 2009. www.who.int.
34. Quoted in World Health Organization, "Healing Child Soldiers."
35. Quoted in Maanvi Singh, "He's 14. He Was a Child Soldier. He's Suicidal. How Can He Be Saved?," NPR, March 11, 2015. www.npr.org.
36. Quoted in *The Business of Giving* (blog), "A Year of Discovery and Renewal in Africa," WordPress, May 2, 2011. https://thebusinessofgiving.wordpress.com.
37. Quoted in Mercy Corps, "Helping Fellow Soldiers Back from Battle: Adriana's Fresh Start," May 11, 2012. www.mercycorps.org.
38. Beah, *A Long Way Gone*, p. 140.
39. Beah, *A Long Way Gone*, p. 149.
40. Beah, *A Long Way Gone*, p. 181.
41. Beah, *A Long Way Gone*, p. 227.

Chapter 5: Addressing the Problem of Child Soldiers

42. Tara Shertel and Joanne Sills, "Healing Through Story: The Effectiveness of Narrative Exposure Therapy for the Treatment of PTSD in Ugandan Ex-Child Soldiers," Rutgers University. http://dialogues.rutgers.edu.

43. Quoted in Singh, "He's 14. He Was a Child Soldier. He's Suicidal. How Can He Be Saved?"

44. Quoted in Singh, "He's 14. He Was a Child Soldier. He's Suicidal. How Can He Be Saved?"

45. Quoted in Gregory Warner, "A Former Child Soldier Will Stand Trial in The Hague for War Crimes," NPR, January 23, 2015. www.npr.org.

46. John Williamson, "The Disarmament, Demobilization and Reintegration of Child Soldiers: Social and Psychological Transformation in Sierra Leone," *Intervention*, 2006. http://our mediaourselves.com.

47. Williamson, "The Disarmament, Demobilization and Reintegration of Child Soldiers."

48. Quoted in Madeline Drexler, "Life After Death: Helping Former Child Soldiers Become Whole Again," Harvard School of Public Health, Fall 2011. www.hsph.harvard.edu.

49. Quoted in Drexler, "Life After Death."

50. Quoted in Michelle Steel, "Child Soldiers," *Vision: Insights and New Horizons,* Fall 2008, www.vision.org.

51. Dallaire, *They Fight like Soldiers, They Die Like Children*, p. 263.

Organizations to Contact

Amnesty International USA
5 Penn Pl., 16th Floor
New York, NY 10001
website: www.amnestyusa.org
e-mail: aimember@aiusa.org

This is a global movement of people dedicated to fighting injustice and promoting human rights. It seeks to investigate and expose human rights abuses, educate the public and mobilize support, and help transform societies to be safer and more just.

International Rescue Committee
122 East Forty-Second St.
New York, NY 10168-1289
website: www.rescue.org
e-mail: communications@rescue.org

This organization is a global humanitarian aid and relief group founded in 1933. It works to restore health, safety, education, and economic well-being to those devastated by military conflict or disaster.

SOS Children's Villages
1620 I St. NW, Suite 900
Washington, DC 20006
website: www.sos-usa.org
email: info@sos-childrensvillages.org

SOS is an international aid organization that cares for more than eighty thousand children in 133 countries. Its mission is to build families for children in need while helping them shape more positive futures and share in the development of their communities.

UNICEF

125 Maiden Ln.
New York, NY 10038
website: www.unicef.org
email: information@unicefusa.org

UNICEF is a humanitarian and development agency that works worldwide for the rights of every child. UNICEF lobbies and partners with government and civilian leaders, thinkers, and policy makers to help gain rights for all children—especially the most disadvantaged.

War Child USA

Times Square
PO Box 668
New York, NY 10108
website: www.warchild.ca
e-mail: info@warchild.ca

This is a nonprofit organization that helps to raise awareness of and support for children affected by war around the world. The group seeks to help children in war-torn communities reclaim their childhood through access to education, opportunity, and justice.

For Further Research

Books

Ishmael Beah, *A Long Way Gone: Memoirs of a Boy Soldier*. New York: Crichton, 2007.

Roméo Dallaire, *They Fight like Soldiers, They Die Like Children: The Global Quest to Eradicate the Use of Child Soldiers*. New York: Walker, 2010.

Peter Eischstaedt, *First Kill Your Family: Child Soldiers of Uganda and the Lord's Resistance Army*. Chicago: Hill, 2013.

Emmanuel Jal and Megan Lloyd Davies, *War Child: A Child Soldier's Story*. New York: St. Martin's, 2010.

Kem Knapp Sawyer, *Grace Akallo and the Pursuit of Justice for Child Soldiers*. Greensboro, NC: Reynolds, 2015.

Internet Sources

Siddharth Chatterjee, "For Child Soldiers, Every Day Is a Living Nightmare," *Forbes*, December 9, 2012. www.forbes.com.

Nick Dorman, "ISIS Using Child Soldiers in Slick and Sick Video to Lure Young British Recruits," *Mirror Online*, June 20, 2015. www.mirror.co.uk.

Brigit Katz, "Female Child Soldiers Can Be Victims of Abuse, Perpetrators of Violence," Women in the World and *New York Times*, August 4, 2015. http://nytlive.nytimes.com.

Maanvi Singh, "He's 14. He Was a Child Soldier. He's Suicidal. How Can He Be Saved?," NPR, March 11, 2015. www.npr.org.

David Smith, "Child Soldiers in Central African Republic More than Doubled, Says Charity," *Guardian* (Manchester), December 17, 2014. www.theguardian.com.

Websites

Children of Conflict: Child Soldiers (www.bbc.co.uk). This BBC website features an overview of the issue of child soldiers, from recruitment and abduction to rehabilitation. The website includes stories, audio links, and links to other sources about child soldiers.

Child Soldiers International (www.child-soldiers.org). This website focuses on all aspects of the issue of child soldiers. Child Soldiers International works for the release of unlawfully recruited children, promotes the successful reintegration of child soldiers into civilian life, and calls for accountability for those who illegally recruit or employ them.

Invisible Children (http://invisiblechildren.com). This website features information about the struggle to end the conflict with Joseph Kony's LRA forces in central Africa and establish a foundation for lasting peace. The site also includes videos that trace the history of the LRA war and profile the notorious warlord Kony.

Red Hand Day Campaign (www.hrw.org/news/2010/01/29/red -hand-day-campaign). This website, part of the Human Rights Watch site, provides information about the Red Hand Day Campaign, which seeks to raise awareness about the problem of child soldier recruitment worldwide. The site also explains how to participate in the annual Red Hand Day commemoration on February 12.

Index

child soldiers from, **49**, **60**
See also Lord's Resistance
  Army
UN Convention on the Rights
  of the Child, 10
United Nations Children's
  Fund (UNICEF), 9, 42, 43,
  45, 72
  on definition of child soldier,
    10
  rehabilitation efforts of, 19,
    58–59

on South Sudan, 27–28
on Yemen, 30

van der Borght, Erwin, 15
Veitch, Jonathan, 27–28

War Child, 11, 72
Williamson, John, 60–61
Win, Tun Tun, 4
Winkler, Nina, 48–49

Yemen, 9, 14, 30

Picture Credits

About the Author

John Allen is a writer who lives in Oklahoma City.